Reaction

Dominik Slusarczyk

ISBN: 978-93-6354-219-8

First Edition: 2024
Rs. 200/-

Cyberwit.net
HIG 45 Kaushambi Kunj, Kalindipuram
Allahabad - 211011 (U.P.) India
http://www.cyberwit.net
Tel: +(91) 9415091004
E-mail: info@cyberwit.net

Printed at Repro India Limited.

Contents

Winter

We will never
Survive this slimming winter.
The ground will get
A bit too hard for our
Flat hands.
The air will get
Too spicy for our
Salty mouths.
Maybe we should just
Sleep until summer.
Grab that candle and
Follow me into a better future.

Sweeter

I broke the bed but
I will fix it with this big stick.
You have to understand that
I am a big man in a little world.
I could fix the sky if I tried.
Watch me make a
Mess of the moon.

Phone

He hangs up.
She
Screams in
Her mind.
She sighs, sits,
Wonders why she
Always picks peasants.
They shine for
A little bit but
Then they get
Horrid and dim.
Maybe she will
Just be single for
One summer.
The right man will
Win big
Before he meets her.
We grow old.
We shrink.
We never get to
Own our own gym.

The Bees

Be the beautiful bees.
They make honey for
The curious children.
The children watch with
Wonder shining in
Their strange smiles.
The bees die.
The children cry.
The honey tastes sour.

Circus

I paid the man twice because
I want twice as much fun.
Look -
There is a big bear in a red wig.
He stands as tall as he can so
He can be as scary as he can.
The little kids laugh.
He roars.
Nobody flinches.
What have those
Bastards done to the poor bear?
Nature should not be a wager we won but
We came, we
Saw, we
Sold it all for a penny.

Eject

We went over there where the
Road ends but
There was nothing there.
You said
There used to be
Bright blue skies right here.
We wandered away without
Ever thinking about keeping the
Dark thoughts out.
You spat at the
Shadows that stalked us like
Predators hating prey.
We will reach the
End of this road next.
There will be nothing there for us so
We will keep travelling like
Cliffs travel into the deep sea.

Ages

The hour has power:
It can make you
Mind your manners and
It can make you
Miss your bus.
You have to
Keep a kind clock close by at all times.
Do not let the
Threats distract you from
Your destiny.
I will set you free so
You can fly with the other
Feathered beasts.
I dream that one day you
Will return the favour by freeing me.

Little Sense

It makes little sense.
I made it with my mind.
Do you see that
The colours crash?
I like the way
The plate of mashed
Potato waited all day.
Do you see that
Each note rings like
Sweet singing?
I like the way
It made me
Make my mistakes.
It makes little sense but
I like it nonetheless.
We were born for
More but
We will die for less.

Our Guns

None of our guns work.
They are leaking -
Stuff keeps coming
Out of the end where
You shoot from.
Maybe we should just resort to
Chucking the bullets at
The sad people.
We will save them from
The lesson of depression.
They will teach us that
You do not have to
Know you will die to
Be able to cry.

Top Hat

Play the
Great game with me.
I made another top hat so
Now we can both be the top hat.
We will roll dice and
Stamp around and
Buy buy buy.
It will be
Like riding
Horses streaming through
The blinding sunshine.
The money doesn't matter even
Though it's how you win;
What matters is the
Top hat is as shiny as
We dream of being.

Your Eyes

Justify your eyes.
They stare where
The fairness of
Fiction is hidden.
Why do you
Choose to charm the
Maids?
They just want to
Churn.
You could be
A builder building mansions
For other people.
You run for fun but
Nobody seems to want
To run with you.
You are alone like
The sun in the sky.

Sticky Seats

This has been the
Worst week of my life.
I thought I'd died but
I woke up in my bed.
The bed was
Hard and cold like
My life was.
I made a big breakfast as
If I had the strength to eat.
I watched TV as if
My mind could still do that.
When I got back in bed I
Prayed for death to get me while I slept.
The next morning I
Woke up again.
God hates me because
I spat in his face when
He offered me salvation.

Never

Never name nature.
When it is
Unknown the
Moon can be massive and
The grass can be
Giants draped in glorious jewellery.
The roses
Know their name is
The same every day but
They will never
Share that simple fact with you.
Let them be
Mysterious.
Choose to fly in
Ignorance.
If you have never heard of
Drowning you
Cannot possibly drown.

Burden

Did your
Dreams come true?
Mine neither.
We should work together.
You get bricks and
I'll mix cement.
We will build our own mansion.
It will have a big pool.
You will not be allowed to swim.
It will have a magnificent bed.
You will not be allowed to sleep.
I have decided that you
Will be the maid.
It doesn't matter:
We are allowed to change that now.
Anybody can be
Anything so
Everybody is eternity.

The Dark Dentist

The hound has
Teeth that hurt like harm.
We need to take him to
The dark dentist.
He has drugs but
He never shares his spoils.
That means he will
Make the dog feel less pain but
The dog will not learn to fly.
Damn that man.
I would only go to him if
I needed to be saved from certain death.

Cute Conquerors

They claim to
Be cute conquerors.
I would let them
Crash my car.
They bound around
The bright mat that
Clashes with their
Singing dreams.
I like the way their
Eyes shine like
Life in the dark.
They smile as if
I am worthy of salvation.
Brave boys.
Glorious girls.
Dead men.
Dying thrills.

Fight

I like it.
You like it.
We fight over it.
I say you
Can have it if
You let me have that
Last gasp of chocolate cake.
You say
I would fight you over
Air if air was worth money.
I spend all day at
Work and don't do a damn thing.
You go to work and
Worship the way the phone rings.
I would sing to you but
You wouldn't understand that the
Sounds combine to make melodies.

Black Socks

Practice matching black socks.
We need you to
Be the best dressed at the dance.
There will be
Boys.
You have to
Turn them into
Toys that make money.
When you grow up you
Will give government grants to
Fat cats.
They will repay you with
Promises they can't seem to keep.

Traps

Give that man a hand.
He dreams of being
Complete like fire.
He has lived his whole
Life as a single slice of a pecan pie.
When men see him they
Think about how they could
Eat him and he would be gone.
He needs to become whole before
Some madman murders him.
Anybody could kill us at
Any moment so we
Pretend everyone we meet is
Our favourite friend.
I counted to ten but
I forgot five existed again.

Vein

That map has a
Little cross over there.
There might be
A measure of treasure.
You want to
Abandon the map?
I guess we could
Crush ice instead.
The summer weather is
Better when you are poorer.
Rich people have to
Hide from the man who
Gives ugly people cancer.
We live outside like
Badgers and rabbits.
Nobody bothers us because
They are scared of our stark bravery.

Sin

Give in to sin.
You can be
Really rich if you
Steal all the sweets in the shop.
You can have
Women if you
Murder a couple of
Cuddly dreams.
Why are you
Helping that old lady with
Her heavy shopping?
Why are you
Teaching that class of
Children maths?
You are not the
Son I won at the summer fair.

Boss

I can't stand that man.
He sits in summer as
If he is the sun.
I understand that
He is really nothing but
Sticky soil.
I try to explain him to
The children but they
Only care about where the
Chocolate is hiding today.
I will write to their
Mothers and tell them everything.
We need to try to be the
People we dream of
Seeing standing as statues.
We need to rise when the
Sky says lie down.

Daisies

The daisies saved
Me from the fire;
I like them like I
Like love.
I will water them every day even
Days when I am sick and sad.
Hopefully they will
Grow into a lovely tree.
I would attach a rope as
Rough as sandpaper then
I would swing happily.
When I swing I will
Understand that we have
The power to make
Flower's dreams a reality.

Lavish

We need you to learn to look:
You must gaze straight at
The day as it races past.
You have to try to catch it before
It is gone for good.
We get a tiny bit of
Time but we waste our
Whole lives trying to fly.
Settle for
Nettles in tea.
Surrender to
Staples in Christmas trees.
You can be the
Dream you dreamed when
You weren't asleep.

The Boar

The boar needs blood.
He will keep
Munching on morsels until
A stunning lightning strike arrives.
He will creep like
Children hiding from
Finding children then
He will run and
Jump at their bad backs.
He kills because he can.
We kill because
We are greedy.
God judges us as
Just as bad as ants eating eyes.

Weapons

The gun knows how to blow but
The knife is wise like bright eyes.
You have to
Choose which chalice to die for.
Would you like to
Shoot or stab?
You can't
Sit or sleep.
We need you for the war that
Is fought over our future.
We want red.
They want dead.
We hit their heads when
They claim to be kings.

Crabs, Beans

He has three beans but
He needs four more.
Do you have the
Manners to help him hunt?
If you catch a crab that
Won't help much but
Then I guess we would
Have a crab as a perfect pet.
Crabs or beans;
Work or sleep.

Get It

You will get it but
It will hate you for
Getting it.
Do you think it
Will really be worth it?
Maybe you
Can have this
Clasping hand instead.
You do not want to
Make it mad.
It will
Hit.
It will
Transform your
Smiles into
Sad.
Have this
Clasping hand instead.
We need to live like
It matters what we do;
The alternative is
Eternal sleep.

In Bins

That bag has a
Big hole in it.
Anything you put in it will
Fall straight out.
We need a
Mother to mend it.
Grab a random woman and
Tell her she is in charge now.
She will order us around and
We will be immensely glad that
We are not to blame anymore.
We can give up control.
We should give up control.
The servants have as
Many ham sandwiches as they
Can cram into their millionaire mouths.
The homeless people are free but
Falling.

Placed

Life likes to lie.
You catch him and ask
Him how he is.
He says
I'm fine,
My friend.

Take

You have to catch that bat:
He is a nightmare wearing black rags.
I hate how he
Hangs from the ceiling.
He is stopping me from
Shopping for blotting paper.
I want him to be
A memory of the fact that
We used to be truly mad.
When I am alone I
Will write a long letter explaining that
I am much better now the
Bat is hanging out with nicer people.

Never Better

I keep getting wet.
Every time I go outside it
Rains on my brain.
I have had enough of
Living like this.
I will buy a
Hat that is full of
Little holes.
I will buy some
Shorts with
Fun flowers on.
It is summer in my mind.
The rain keeps falling but
I am soaring through shorter skies.

Ship

I paid yesterday to go away.
When tomorrow comes I
Will finally be able to sail my ship.
It has sails that
Catch cute winds.
It has planks that
Shine like life.
It has a big wheel.
When I turn the wheel I
Will imagine myself as a captain.
We are in charge of
Ourselves and nothing more.

Lower

Do not dig there:
There is only
Soil there.
You have to dig beside
That big tree:
You will find
Diamonds and gold.
We will get rich when
We know enough stuff.
I will teach you ten facts as
Long as you keep growing.
We went to the show but
We couldn't see the stars.

Best Dress

That light is
A bit bright but
I like it nonetheless.
I will let it
Light my life while
I dress in my best dress.
When I am perfect I
Will stride through sunburnt cities.
The people who
See me will be
Pleased to have seen me.
They will not get
The goal.
I follow fools because I
Am scared of making my own mistakes.

Group

I want my
Bones to be bigger.
There are many mountains that
Are a little bit taller than me.
There are rivers that are
So deep I cannot
Wander through them.
If I was a giant I
Would love life like
Birds love flight.
If I was a giant I
Would sing sweet songs about
How the summer sun shines bright.
I pray to God.
God says
Be happy with
Sanity.
I pray to the devil.
The devil says
Greed is a necessity.
We desperately need to
Want the world.
Take everything they have.
Take everything they have.
They will only ruin it by
Allowing it to be free.

The Wet Wood

Should I
Let the wet wood win?
He claims to be the
King of the field.
I call him
Crashing cars.
His mind is bright but
Baskets break too.
We compete.
I steal his seat.
He says he
Likes using his
Thin feet anyway.
One day we will
All be big winners.
Follow the man
Following the man
Following the stars.

Reality Weeps

We need to breathe.
The bad man is sitting outside our
Sad door.
What does he want?
He will kill.
What do we do?
We debate killing but
Decide murdering is
Hurtling over the cliff.
I refuse to be bad like him.
We drink giant glasses of gin and
Thank God for making doors.
The bad man will get bored and
Wander away.
We just need to
Be brave for one more day.

Diamond

Do you want to
Do it too?
We can be
Brothers.
We will fight the
War together.
The weather won't
Ever force us apart.
We share a bond.
We shared a bond.
I spit at you while
You scream at me.
We can be
Brothers but
Not sisters.

High Hats

The gems bend the light.
I can see straight through to
The other side of the curtain.
There are people there.
They might be big or
They might be small.
All I can see is they are
Dark.
I will put the gems back in
The black case.
If I ever take them out
Again it will be because I
Have given up.
Knowledge is never nice.
We live under a sky that
Doesn't know our names.

Temperature

This is when your life ends.
Don’t cry, my child.
You had a lovely life.
Your mother taught you manners.
Your father taught you how
To tame fire.
Your wife taught you
How and why to use the knife.
You must
Abandon every one of them now.
Walk with me.
We will travel across the
Sea and meet the
Jesus who chats with the Jews.

Quality

Get a head.
Lose the head.
Pretend you never
Knew which way to walk.
They tried to teach us
How to act but we
Said we didn't want to be actors.
We want millions of pounds to
Just appear in our accounts.
Playful people keep
Making us work in sad shirts.
We will work when
Working is fighting in tights.
I had a head and
I will have a head again.

Water

I never needed water;
I only needed hugs.
You are bright like a butterfly's life.
You light up my night sky.
I would follow you into
Any flickering fire however
Ferocious it was.
The smoke will make me
Choke but I will keep
Striding and smiling anyway.
I would follow you up
Any mountain.
The air will be thin like
Sin and I will
Struggle to breathe but
I will stride and smile while
You rush on ahead.
I never needed water but
I beg for a sip on my death bed.

That Gun

Grab that gun:
You have to
Shoot that soldier or
He will shoot you.
It is like a
Computer game but
When you die you
Die in real life.
Maybe the cloud land will
Be as comfortable as cash.
It is better but
It is worse but
I guess we will die anyway.

Murder

It is murder.
They claim to be
Conquerors but
We see that they
Are really conjurors.
You could help but
It would be hard.
You do not want to help?
I curse the
Children you cherish.

Suffering

Sometimes suffering stops.
You have to
Stay alive all night in case you
Become Big Ben.
Some say life is easy but
We are so needy and
The greedy people steal the real deals.
All we want is to
Not have to work.
Nobody really wants the money;
They just want the light to
Shine out of somebody else's mind.

House

Every man has
A house.
Some houses are
Big buckets and
Some houses are
Small snails.
Would you like to
Try to find your house?
Someone must have
Made a map once.
Find the map then
Find the house then
Find out why the
House is hollow.

The Parched Pack

We cannot get ahead of
The parched pack.
They have been chasing us for
Days because they need our clean clothes.
We must try to
Lose them in the light or
They will maim us in the dark.
Flee from life with me.
We were born free so
We ran from our
Responsibilities as fast as
Numbers change and become higher.

Cancer

He will never get better.
He is doomed to die like
Yesterday died when
Today invaded.
Today understands that soon
He will die too.
The days ravage each other like
The cancer has ravaged this man's body.
He did everything he was supposed to do.
He didn't smoke for a second.
He never went in the sun once.
He ate apples and
Oranges and pears.
Cancer doesn't care.
Today will die when
Tomorrow decides the
Time is just right.
We are sat on the bus but
We're not allowed to stand on the bus.

Jolly Gems

That man is Santa.
He brings us
Pretty presents but
Only if we are good food.
We will say
Please and thank you to
Everybody we meet.
The stupid people smile at us.
We scowl in our minds.
Life is not that nice when
You are living a lie.
We will trick that
Bastard into giving us
Shiny knives and guns that bang.

Brothers

I pressed play.
You pressed pause.
We fought over which
Button to press next.
You are a brother who
Bashes bullies with sticks.
I am a brother who
Waits for you at the gate every day.
We stride straight towards the sunrise because
We are not scared of the light.
Our mother worries but we
Are safe because we
Are together like treasure.
Forever.
Forever.
I write my name in the stars and
Explain the language to you and only you.

Learn With Me

Learn with me.
We will be
Blue boys in
Blue skies.
They will be
Green girls in
Glittering dresses.
One day we will
Grow into giants as
Tall as tumbling towers.
People will ask us
How we did it.
We will say
Learn with me.

Tiles

They played the same game but
One man lost and one man won.
What are we to do about
The fact that winning creates losers?
Maybe we should settle for
Simply sitting on sofas all day.
If we try we might
Become much worse.
When the hearse comes for
Me I am dressed in my best suit.
They are playing violins but
I can only hear sobbing.

Exam

We need to
Be way better.
We will
Work harder for longer.
We will
Stay inside even when
The summer sun is
Lovely and light.
I am going to
Learn every fact this
Brown book has
Stacked in it.
When the exam comes I
Will write my name.
If that is not
Enough I didn't want
A certificate anyway.

Statistics

They say
Statistics hit it.
I say
Run away from
My flying eyes.
The statistics say
Men are only
Men when
Winter wins the war.
The men pick up
Poorly pens and
Write nice new lies.
They say they are stories.
I call them
Glory soaked in
Stinking mud.
The statistics win because
I can't count past one.

Kittens

We banned books.
Everybody has to
Stare at screens all day now.
Nobody wants to
Be a writer anymore.
Good:
They would surely have failed anyway.
Now everybody wants to
Be an actress.
I feel they will fail at that like
Lambs fail to fly through blue skies.
Why do we want?
The sun is beautiful but
If we stroked it we would
Burn and die.

The Song

Is the song wrong or
Are we actually as
Deaf as dead frogs?
I used to be able to
Smooth out the moving tunes;
Now I can't
Crash into the bristling
Beat however much it wobbles.
I will go to sleep.
Maybe when I wake up I
Will be young again.

Freedom

Freedom means you
Need to fight at
The exact right time.
Fight the man who
Says you have to work.
Fight the woman who
Says you have to
Clean your clothes.
Fight the child who says
She is hungry.
We will win when
Everyone else is either
Crying or dead.

Underneath Chaos

I expect death.
I get regret.
My sofa is soft but
It does not make me
Feel any better.
I want a chunk of chocolate cake.
I want the
Aches to fly away to yesterday.
I want to not
Remember.
Everything I did I did wrong.
I wrote a song for
Deaf people.
They danced because they
Pitied me.

Spot

I got us a
Spot at the
Hottest spot in town.
We will eat
Big burgers and
Chunky chips.
It will be
Bliss simmering in a
Glowing pan.
I will watch you
Eat and wonder why
You choose to eat with me.
I was never Jesus;
I am ordinary like
Ash on pants.
Maybe you are
Using me for money.
Maybe I am not as
Ugly as my brothers told me.
I like you because
You like me.

www.ingramcontent.com/pod-product-compliance
Lightning Source LLC
LaVergne TN
LVHW090136160826
845673LV00017B/2487
9789363542198